THE
FIVE BUDDHIST
PRECEPTS

Brian Taylor

UNIVERSAL OCTOPUS

Other Publications in the
Basic Buddhism Series

What is Buddhism?
The Living Waters of Buddhism
Buddhism and Drugs
Basic Buddhist Meditation
Basic Buddhism for a World in Trouble
Dependent Origination (*Paṭiccasamuppāda*)
The Ten Fetters (*Saŋyojana*)
The Five Nivāraṇas (*Buddha's Teaching
of the Five Hindrances*)
Buddhist Pali Chants with English Translations

Published by Universal Octopus 2018
www.universaloctopus.com

ISBN 978-1-9999063-6-8

CONTENTS

I undertake to observe the precept
to abstain from killing living beings.

I undertake to observe the precept
to abstain from taking things not given.

I undertake to observe the precept
to abstain from misuse of the senses.

I undertake to observe the precept
to abstain from false speech.

I undertake to observe the precept
to abstain from drinks and drugs
causing heedlessness.

THE FIVE BUDDHIST PRECEPTS

All that we are is the product of what has been done. What we will become is the product of what we are doing now.

Everything is done in the present. The present is like a moving point or wave of activity, travelling through time and space.

Although the products of the past are all around us, the past itself has gone. Nothing can be done in the past. As for tomorrow, we can do nothing there until it becomes today.

If we understand this, we see how supremely important it is to do only those things *now* that produce results in the future which are wholly satisfactory. The future is our future. It is we who will inherit the results of our todays.

How shall we decide what to do? And what not to do? The best guide is ourselves. *We should not do to others what we do not want to be done to us.*

Since we want to be happy, we should not impair the happiness of others.

It is on this basis that the Five Buddhist Precepts are constructed. These are intentions, promises, which one makes to oneself. They act as a restraining framework within which our activities take place.

1. **I undertake to observe the precept to abstain from killing living beings.**

2. **I undertake to observe the precept to abstain from taking things not given.**

3. **I undertake to observe the precept to abstain from misuse of the senses[1].**

4. **I undertake to observe the precept to abstain from false speech.**

5. **I undertake to observe the precept to abstain from drinks and drugs causing heedlessness.**

1. One wants to live. One does not want to die. This is fundamental. Other living beings are the same. They struggle to survive, as any hunter, fisherman, farmer or entomologist

---

[1] *See NOTES page 15*

knows. In a well-known reading book for very young children it used to say, "Cows give us their milk." They don't. We take it. It is the same with their lives. We take their bodies. Because we want to eat them. If *we* don't want to be killed ourselves, we should keep the first precept and say that we are not going to kill *others*.

2. With Stealing it's simple. It causes me inconvenience when someone steals *my* wallet or my car or even my book, so I decide not to steal what belongs to *him*. Of course you will meet a man who says that, ultimately, nobody can own anything. Philosophically, he may have a point. But the chances are he has his eye on somebody's something. So, keep your hands in your pockets while he's around!

3. This Third Precept is often understood by later Buddhists, especially in the West, as referring to Sexual Misconduct. Obviously, this can be seen as part of it. If you run off with someone else's wife or husband, it causes suffering and often breaks up someone's family as well. If you sleep around without the knowledge of your partner or the other person's partner, it is a breach of trust that can cause a lot of pain. If a relationship doesn't work, it's cleaner just to terminate it. Start again. Without deception.

4. If you don't refrain from False Speech, if you tell someone something that isn't true, the very least you will cause him is inconvenience.

If we put ourselves in the position of those who are on the receiving end of these actions - who are killed, whose possessions are stolen, who are betrayed by their wives or husbands or sexually abused, who are deceived by the lies and untruths of others - then we will not want to cause that suffering to others.

5. As for the Fifth Precept, our society is full of broken lives and human disasters that are the results of alcohol and drug abuse. Crime, road accidents, poverty, broken homes, violence, physical illness, mental illness and misery.

The Fifth Precept is aimed at substances like alcohol, cannabis, opium (and its derivative heroin), cocaine, mescalin, amphetamines,

LSD etc. In the Buddha's own time it would have included soma, about which so much is written in Vedic literature.

Why does a Buddhist undertake to abstain from these things? Because they lead to carelessness.

Carelessness leads to mistakes.

Buddhism teaches Karma, cause and effect. If this, then that. If not this, then not that. In dealing with things, Buddhism seeks out the causes. If you change the cause, the effect changes automatically. If, on the other hand, you merely remove the effects and leave the cause untouched, that same cause will produce more effects of the same kind.

You cut the weeds. They grow again. If you want to get rid of them altogether, you have to dig out their roots.

The cause of taking alcohol and drugs is that, when first experimented with, one likes what they do to one's body and mind.

One feels exhilarated, excited, ecstatic even.

One has a feeling of well-being or of greater self-confidence. Or it helps to overcome, or even temporarily disperse altogether, thought or memories that are painful or worrying. In short it makes one feel better.

But in the long term it turns out to be more like a bait, which ensnares the fish.

Inside the bait is a hook!

The desirable experiences fade. This makes it necessary to take more. Two pints instead of one. Two pills. Two joints. Still the pleasure diminishes. The doses increase. The pleasure does not.

Stronger drugs are needed. Cocaine and opium replace cannabis. Heroin replaces cocaine. LSD replaces amphetamines. Whisky and vodka replace beer.

The decrease in pleasure is accompanied by a corresponding increase in the negative effects. The body becomes increasingly unwell with nausea, pains in the joints and muscles, headaches, fever, loss of appetite, difficulty in sleeping, a serious weakening of the immune system.

At this stage, one is drinking and taking drugs not for pleasure, but in order to get a momentary respite from suffering. One is seriously ill.

Inevitably, one's relationships suffer. One finds it difficult to keep a job. Money becomes a serious problem because, as one finds it harder to earn it, the costs of buying alcohol or drugs in the quantities needed for even temporary relief escalate. It is a bleak picture.

Rehabilitation is difficult. Withdrawal symptoms are severe. One hundred percent recovery is uncommon. Often the optimum result is "containment". This means that the patient is kept relatively stable by prescribed "safe" drugs. "Relatively stable" does not mean he is happy, healthy and enjoying a good life. It means that, while on the medication (which will always have its own side-effects) he may be less of a social problem to others.

Quite commonly, there is a relapse. A return to drinking and drug-taking. The destructive cycle repeats itself. Mind and body are weakened, and serious illness and consequent death are often the result.

It is not only the individual who is affected. The effects on his or her family are devastating. For children, to grow up in a family where there is drink or drug abuse is a terrible start to life.

Of course, prevention is better than cure. But it seems clear that the drug education programmes in schools aren't entirely successful.

Their efforts are not helped by the entertainment artists who target the young. They are often alcoholics and drug takers themselves and contribute to a drug culture as role models. The sad fact is that the entertainment industry makes a lot of money and is very powerful.

At the present time, it is not possible for a democratic government to confront all of the unwholesome propaganda which targets the young and vulnerable. Assuming that it had the will to do so.

Certainly, in the western democracies, punitive legislation has not worked.

If the water pipe is leaking, the effect is pools of water. If you spend your time mopping up the water with a cloth, you will work for a long time. To solve the problem you must find the cause of the leak and mend it.

With Buddhism, this simple logical approach is applied to everything.

Primarily, it is applied to the fact of suffering. If you wish to escape from suffering you must remove the cause of suffering. If you want to avoid the consequences of alcohol or drug addiction, leave them alone.

SMOKAJOINTA

They say it's bad for for you, don't you?

Brian

These substances lead men to carelessness about their own bodies, which become sick and degenerate. Their judgement becomes impaired so that they make mistakes in handling their personal affairs, in their work, in their driving, in their relationships with others. If they have families and dependents, these too are affected by the errors of judgement resulting from this carelessness.

This carelessness is avoided if the *cause,* the drug itself, is given up and avoided.

How does the type of carelessness that results from drug taking work?

Drugs dominate a man's mind and body. This causes him to lose the power of sane and rational judgement, of vigilance.

As a result of this, he makes mistakes.

It is easy to see, therefore, that 'drugs' that can do this don't only grow in the earth as plants or come out of the chemist's laboratory as pills. They can come just as readily from between the covers of a book or a television screen or from speakers of a radio or a computer.

As an escape from reality, which is what drink and drug abuse is, books, entertainment and music are widely used. As any schoolboy knows.

For us, the important thing is to *apply* cause and effect. These things cause suffering to oneself and others. These things I will abstain from. No cause. No effect. No drink or drugs. No carelessness. No consequences.

If we were wholeheartedly to adopt these five precepts and live our lives by them, we would no longer cause suffering to other living beings by our actions.

In this way we would normalise our relationships with others and the world around us. The internal Path can now be trodden with a minimum of interference.

Our consciences would become clearer. Although the things that we have done in the past would still cast their shadows on the present, the shadows themselves would fade and we would derive much encouragement from this.

KEEPING THE PRECEPTS

Yet keeping these precepts is the outer shell of morality. It means one is restraining oneself from doing these things.

But if one is restraining oneself, it indicates that there is something to be restrained.

When one investigates this, one can see that before every act of killing, stealing, misuse of the senses, lying and drinking or taking drugs, there is a *mental* impulse to do these things. So long as these mental impulses arise, one cannot be sure that they will never lead to action.

The next step is to purify the mind so that negative or unwholesome states will never arise in us again.

Purifying the mind is similar to weeding a garden. You decide which plants are weeds and pull them out. And you encourage the good plants.

When this is achieved, human beings will have reached the first stage of human completeness or human perfection.

Or, to put it another way, human beings will be back to normal.

If these precepts were kept throughout the human world, it would make an unbelievable difference. There would be no war, no serious crime, and no need for money to be spent on armies, policing, courts of justice or prisons.

NOTES

This is the Third Precept *(see page 2):*

Kāmesumicchācārā veramanī sikkhāpadam samādiyāmi.

I undertake to abstain from misuse of the senses.

Kāmesumicchācārā, literally and originally, means: *misuse of the senses.* That is, any of the senses. Later, it acquired the more limited meaning of sexual misconduct. This is variously interpreted by different cultures and in different places. Misleadingly, it has acquired the status of a standard English translation.

Of course, it can include adultery and paedophilia. But it is not only misuse of sexual desire. It is misuse of <u>any</u> senses contacting their sense objects and setting up a state of interactive pollution with the mind.

Think of those Roman gluttons who, having eaten as much as they could, vomited it all up and returned for more! Think of youngsters with earphones on full blast to shut out the world. Think of Cleopatra and her vials of perfume and daily baths in fresh asses' milk. Think of drunkenness, drug addiction, body piercing, masochism. Think of uncontrolled thinking.

THE QUIET MIND

The Sun
shines
in a bucket of water
and doesn't
get wet.

CPSIA information can be obtained
at www.ICGtesting.com
Printed in the USA
BVHW071801090922
646655BV00011B/884